Bedside Diary

a collection of poems by
Matthew Aaron

This edition designed by Ari Choquette

Cover image by kayepants
(Flickr Creative Commons license)

To Becky, Linda, Reba and Wilma.
The original "Golden Girls".

Contents

Forgotten Maiden • *1*

Stone Cold Sober • *2*

Black Waters • *4*

Missing You • *5*

Night Pal • *7*

Slipping Away • *8*

Stages • *10*

Goodbye • *11*

Bedside Diary • *12*

Frightened Child • *14*

the chill of a faded whisper • *16*

The Passage • *18*

Now It's My Turn • *20*

Fracture • *21*

Willing Sacrifice • *23*

Resurrection • *25*

I Died Today • *26*

Images • *27*

Familiar Strangers • *28*

eyes of sovereignty • *29*

The Guardian • *31*

Reassurance • *32*

A Cure For Writer's Block • *33*

Fantasy • *35*

Midwater Madness • *37*

Redemption • *39*

Reminisce • *41*

Samson's Song • *42*

Hibernation • 43

Who Do You Trust? • 45

Cutting the Cord • 46

Severance • 47

Back Porch Recollections • 48

Remembrance • 50

Demise in the Face of Freedom • 53

Never Love Again • 55

Sunrise Confessions • 56

The Passion of Regret • 57

Walls • 58

Ship Lights • 60

Dual Personality • 61

Save the Wounded Souls • 62

The Lake • 63

Fraternal Disorder • 64

Do You Love Me • 66

Alias • 69

Anger (Under New) Management • 70

In Silence Comes My Energy • 72

Passing Through • 74

Shattered • 76

Blind Ambition • 77

Release • 79

First Love • 80

Thanks Mom • 81

Free • 82

The Search • 83

Mental Gymnastics • 84

Revenge • 85

Freeze Warning • *86*

Brotherly Love • *87*

Lost Child • *88*

Last Curtain Call • *90*

House of My Sorrow • *92*

The Ritual • *94*

Mediocrity Personified • *96*

I Have Seen the Face of God • *97*

My Angel • *98*

Bringing Together of a Few • *100*

Rubble • *101*

Massacred Emotions • *103*

Assassin • *105*

Piracy • *107*

Rise and Fall • *108*

Game of Chance • *110*

Decisions • *112*

The Presence • *113*

Rise Up: A message from a loving Father • *115*

Reluctant Hero • *116*

Simple Solution • *118*

The Hero • *120*

Notes • *122*

"You intended to harm me, but God intended it for good to accomplish what is now being done, the saving of many lives."

—*Genesis 50:20*

Welcome to the most random collection of poetry. I use the word "collection" loosely. The only commonality with these poems is that they came to rest in the same book. Dilemma. What do you call such a haphazard, literary gathering; "Random Freakish Thoughts"? Although descriptively accurate, it seems a little superficial. I chose instead, "Bedside Diary". It captures more of the intimate, personal feel of these writings.

The name "Bedside Diary" was originally the title of a poem I wrote a long time ago. I decided to use the name for this book, because the diversity of the writing is something akin to the random thoughts one would scribble on a nightstand notepad, in those closing moments of the day, shortly before bed. These poems cover every aspect of my life: sex, suicide, fear, despair, hatred for my father, reconciliation with my father, tales of my gay life, tales of my straight life and eventually how God redeemed every last crazy moment.

I started writing poetry as young man. A somewhat dysfunctional family provided me with plenty of material. Writing was the "pressure release valve" that ensured my pain never reached feverish levels. As a kid, I was happier with a virgin piece of paper than a new toy. I could escape into a world where pen and paper reigned supreme. Poetry gave my pain safe passage into the world, allowing me to heal from the effects of unbridled emotions.

As my gift developed, my writing took on an empathetic nature. Eventually, I was writing poetry about other people's trials. The poem that is the namesake of this book is loosely based on an actual suicide note. In college, the best friend of the guy I was dating committed suicide, leaving behind two young children.

Her note was pointed and simple.

Since that time I have written many other pieces based on the stories of people in my life. This collection contains poems from the part of my life that brought me to the place where I handed control of my life over to Jesus Christ. Many in today's world might consider me to have been born gay. I choose to believe that I was born sensitive, artistic and creative. I don't believe anyone is born gay. That is a statement based on my life experience not prejudice.

I tried for a long time to make life work on my own terms. I failed a lot. Not having found salvation in my sexuality, guys, possessions or even my childhood dream, I walked away from homosexuality in 1998 and returned to the God of my youth for direction. I have held nothing back. These are the poetic ramblings of my lowdown, dirty existence and the God who cleaned me up.

My life has been uniquely random. This book is an introspective exercise of many years of struggle, triumph and vision.

Bedside Diary

☀

Forgotten Maiden

She covers herself.
The night air,
more than cool,
cuts through the weathered fibers of the quilt;
a frozen blade,
serrated by rust and time.
The final dagger comes
as the warmth of the sun
is ripped away.
Pain pulses below the surface,
settling beneath her skin,
tethering itself to her soul.
When the last rays of sun tease her with only light,
tears began to fall.
The liquid warms her cheeks.
Bowing her head,
she remembers the way home,
accepting death's icy embrace.

Stone Cold Sober

The rock sat quietly,
longing for a dip in the fluorescent pool.
It would always be this far from the water.
A quiet sentinel,
this was its place in the world.
It wished only for a heavy tide or
a fierce wind,
to issue forth a taste of the blue magic.
It dreamed of executing a beautiful swan dive or
even a chaotic belly flop.
All were inconceivable.
Stationary it would remain.
Nestled forever on the shore:
a remnant of a cliff,
the seedling of a mountain,
decoration for all to see.
In the still evening,
an outstretched arm to the water's edge,
all but a dream.
The rock had no hands.
Its only distinguishing features,
layers of clay upon limestone.
Dull reds.
Whispered browns.
Faded ribbons of gold,
the only hint of its regal aspirations.
Its etched surface
adorned with petrified leaves and

ancient fossilized imagery.
Once,
among the fissures,
a lone arachnid had crossed.
The rock marveled at the tiny one's precious gift of movement.
A treasured art form.
Somewhere among the lines,
crevices and
fractures,
one could almost detect,
a smile.

Black Waters

Bathed in color
I fight to maintain my ground
As I sink
   brilliant hues disappear
The blues remain
My faithful companion envelopes me
Structures around me
   immersed in the liquid matrix
Life is
   washed of character
   stripped of its voice
Rocks
   baptized and alive
   ascend from the depths
   forming the backdrop of my demise
Events play out
   too far down to find my way back
I endeavor to fight
   summon the colors I covet
   restore them to my new world
   give vision back to the mind
Descending further
   all light dwindles
My sapphire savior forsakes me

... black waters flood my soul

Missing You

Each night I go to bed,
I wish tonight would be the last.
Last time I sleep and dream of you,
And think about our past.
Doomed to see forever,
the face I loved so dear.
Tormented and anguished,
in solitary fear.
A truer picture of myself,
I'll probably never find.
Remembering how good it felt,
That your life ransomed mine.
Images and objects,
Slowly come to view.
Then right before my very eyes,
They morph and become you.
Erotic dreams. Romantic scenes.
I wish they'd all just go.
For each time I revisit us,
I feel my longing grow.
The pictures are so real you see,
Words you said are true.
I close my eyes and hold my breath
And wish for love anew.
You're far away, long since gone,
Forgotten where we were.
When last you pledged your love to me,

And let those feelings stir.
Memories are what they say,
We'll have until we die.
I'd settle for just one last kiss,
One final, sad goodbye.

Night Pal

I sit
quietly watching
black clouds
seep from the cracks of heaven
I smile
darkness bathes the sky
choking out the last reds of the sunset
The sun
mysteriously ripped from the horizon
sleeps under lock and key
held captive by the force
that steals my world from sight
I imagine
nightfall
my old friend
adorned in his ebony cloak
sitting beside me
on the green carpet of the lawn
I feel secure
my true self surrendered to the darkness
For it has no voice
but listens to mine

Slipping Away

She heard a door slam,
labored footsteps followed.
Safety,
still a breath away,
her hand came to rest on a shelf in the closet.
The only light,
filtered in through the crack in the doors.
She clinched her eyelids tight,
warding off evil with every blink.
The shuffling grew closer.
Soon it would venture into her hiding place,
devouring her in this makeshift tomb.
A light bulb ruptures,
glass shards rain down.
Luminescent energy is surrendered to the darkness.
It is now in the room
near the bed.
Pitch black surroundings,
improve it's hunting skills.
Aware of her pounding heart,
breaths fell in rhythmic interludes of panic.
Blood oozes from a wounded foot.
She scuttled backwards,
as the doors are murderously coaxed from their sockets.
Mortality permeates the air,
sensing her fear,
probing the darkness with elevated rapture.
To no avail she scurries to one side.

It pursues,

hunger increasing.

Pinned against the wall of the closet,

she rests.

Evil is upon her.

Hopeless screams disappear into overhanging garments.

Bones crack.

Matchsticks in the hands of a giant.

Pain gives way to oblivion.

As she fades,

she glimpses piercing, green eyes,

and a toothy grin that's somehow familiar.

Stages

I see you there,
hiding in the fear I find familiar.
I see you there,
struggling to save yourself.
I see you there,
in my shoes,
running for your sanity.
I remember myself as you are now.
Memories taunt me with wicked anticipation.
The innocence of the discovery.
The horror and shame of the knowledge.
I see you there
and weep quietly to myself.
Despair,
a hot acid,
eating away from the inside.
Viral emotions invade my soul.
I see you there.
Blind faith tells me you will be fine.
The author of your life will grant the happy ending
for which we had all hoped.
After a while though,
you'll stop fighting.
When the stars seem to fade,
their brilliant intensities no longer a worthwhile goal.
Fear of the unknown subsides.
Yet nothing is scarier,
than surrender.

Goodbye

I'm leaving now
I've been ready for a long time
You haven't been ready for me to go
And that's fine
I won't tell you not to cry
Not to be sad
Remember the times we shared
The loved ones I leave behind
I was truly blessed
A long life was my gift
Time well spent
I could never imagine my death
Any more than you could
God has shown me the way
As I go gently into the grand scape of another world
Remember me
When you cry
Your tears shall echo in the great halls of heaven
And I will know
You loved me.

Bedside Diary

After this I'm not a mother...
After this I'm nothing.

When my body is over,
The life I've led gone through.
Understand,
I still love you.
I leave you my memory,
my eternal, vivid soul.
I tell you that I'm sorry
and send you on your way.
With all my heart I loved you.
My life was built for you.
I can't go on any longer.
The foundations of my heart bleed,
for my children,
   my soul,
    lost hope.
All my life I pulled everyone closer to my soul,
drenching them in liquid laughter.
Now my cup runs dry.
   No more cries of laughter
   will echo in my ears.
   All I have and all I know
   is written in these tears.
   As I end a life of heartache,
   I end a life of pain.

I stand beside the waters
and let my troubles drain

After this I'm not a mother...
After this I'm nothing.

...a white, linen, night cloth in a state of disarray.

Frightened Child

He sits quietly by himself,
a scared child older than I.
I only want to help.
Who am I to offer comfort in his confusion?
I lend an ear.
I give my time.
I want his undying love.
The child sits motionless,
unable to give.
He doesn't understand.
His only instinct,
take,
survive.
He can offer nothing.
He moves toward me, with stiffness lacking emotion.
Fluidity of movement drained by sedentary pain.
Speaking softly,
hidden ears may tell of his tales,
    "I don't know what to do."
I listen.
    "I don't know where to go."
I understand.
    "I don't know wrong from right."
I cry.

I offer a kind word.
I possess no solutions or understanding.
The answers he needs,

lie somewhere beneath the fractures
time has etched in the delicate glasswork of his mind.
One last try.
I reach out to hold his troubled soul, with a smile.
Touch is no good.
He can't be reached physically.
As my prayers go out for a miracle,
access to his world wanes.
Emotional ties fade.

the chill of a faded whisper

They speak to me each morning
Voices heard each day
Some sing a song of rapture
Some bow their heads to pray

Little ones come running
Elders keep at bay
Watching as I enter
My presence parts the way

I carry out my calling
A tradition handed down
Another steps into the realm
Intruders all around

All are cloaked and hooded
Foreigners to this harsh land
Soon the sun shall rise again
The dawn is close at hand

The ritual soon over
Morning hours pass
Strangers bring the gifts again
The Elders reserve won't last

Leaving sacred Holy Lands
The pilgrims make their way
Sharing and rejoicing
For the offering this day

Black and White united
Color plays a role
Always for protection
Evil lurks below

One by one they savor
A meal that's fit for Kings
Soon the sun climbs higher
The little ones now sing

Some enjoy the water
Taking in a swim
Others find a greater reward
Diving deep within

The evening hour approaches
Foreigners have gone
A chill ushers forth the darkness
Whispers replace the song

The Passage

You passed from this world
I felt you go
Our connection slipped away
The light faded from your eyes
A brilliant sunset disappeared
Your spirit made its way towards heaven
As you passed from this world
A part of my soul went with you
Insuring your happiness
And mine
Tears fell with emotional clarity
I close my eyes
For my light too has faded
Each time death came knocking
You opened not the door
Cherished ones went walking
Along a foreign shore
You watched them as they waded
Friends will come and go
You stayed behind and listened
Watched the waters roll
Ripples on the surface
Words I never spoke
Others went before you
Memories evoked

We shared much more than laughter
My solitary friend
Immerse yourself in freedom
Don't let the demons win

Now It's My Turn

At silent still times in life
she would sit alone
watching the blue magnet of the morning sky
smiling as it pulled her close.
She found refuge
in comfortable clouds
secreting away her emotions in their billowy whiteness.
She longed to sit for hours
soaking up the
friendly
cleansing
arrows of sunlight.
Lounging on the emerald blanket of the lawn
a tin
blue willow
tea cup nestled beside her.
She wished that she was somewhere
over that broad spectrum of life
where the air was free of
  baking cookies
    screaming grandchildren
the raspy whining of the bingo auctioneer.
She needed
a place to sit
drink sweet amaretto tea
and age at her own pace.

Fracture

I remember when we were just a woman and a boy.
All we had was each other.
All we had was our love.
Now you are a man.
I stand alone.
A saddened soul in a withered body.
Your letters explain
why you feel we've grown apart.
All I know is that you are not here.
You are not my little boy any more.
That simple thought makes me sad.
The space at my side will never again be filled.
Sometimes I close my eyes tight,
not to wish you back,
but to picture scenes from your childhood,
to capture emotions behind the laughter.
I could offer you nothing but love.
That is all I have now.
I need you.
You have your dreams.
I love you,
but feel the need for distance,
to spare myself more pain
and give you the space to fly.
You were my only joy in life.
My one, true source of happiness.
As the light of your life burns in the distance,
I hope you can see only my hand waving goodbye.

The tears are for my eyes only.
For they aren't tears at all.
Deep down inside,
I know my soul is melting.

Willing Sacrifice

You hear a mystic whisper,
A mist comes through the trees.
A maiden and her damsels,
Are forced onto their knees.

The dragon's lair is baited,
Gifts of flesh and blood.
Rain pours down from heaven,
Waters churn and flood.

They know their lives are ending,
To save a chosen few.
Death creeps 'round about them,
The devil takes his cue.

Wings of golden sinew,
Scales of diamond shard.
Fire pours forth from evil,
A demon plays its card.

Circling round the bounty,
An offering of peace.
With skillful execution,
He savors his royal feast.

When all the bones are broken,
Blood no longer flows.
The armor-plated specter
Slithers back to shadow.

Resurrection

The sky opened up and a rain fell
Coating the structures of the farm with a luminous glaze
Cool wetness poured new life into the old forms
The pungent smell of spring permeated the air
As the earth uttered a collective sigh
Fresh water cleansed its pores
Pools of the sustaining liquid
Began to form
Tiny rivers carved out hash marks in the soil
Thunderous drops awakened the
Remaining mounds of earth
Clods lost their cohesive hold
Crumbling under the persuasive notions of the water
Raindrops danced and rolled down the roof of the barn
Heralding their arrival to the eager ground below
Wood fences drank in the foreign moisture
Who knew when this heavenly beverage would be offered
again?

I Died Today

I gave you my soul gentle one
You gave me sorrow
You severed my life from the living
I died today
A wind driven slave
Thrown off course by your love
Can you live with my betrayal?
My lifeless form will be reborn
A slaying on your blood soaked hands
Daggers with pristine blades skim the edges of my existence
Freeing me of the hope I have
My trust
A trophy you wear with pride
You feasted on all my emotions
Leaving me rotted and cored
Never again will I feel anguish
I am invincible now
Your lessons learned well
I seek the shelter of exile
To peer into the fire
Kill the phoenix as it arises
Consume its mighty essence
Until I am strong enough
To drink of yours
I died today
But time calls me on
To a battle I will not lose again

Images

By such air that angels fly
Demons also spread their wings
The life left behind will go on forever

By such air that man breathes life
Death may also cloud his lungs
The lives left behind will grieve forever

By such powers that build mountains high
Valleys appear as rifts in the great scape
The void left behind an endless reminder

By such mindless mistakes that go unseen
Thousands utter their last breath
Scathing war cries piercing the realm of eternity

Familiar Strangers

I sit casually eyeing the dawn of a new day
From my vantage point
I see others gathered here
More than the stirring beauty of this place
or the opportunity of renewal it provides
they are here for me
Gauging my reaction
Feeding off the energy it generates in me
Unwelcome settlers to my homeland
Fear
like a wild vine
attempts to choke out my drive to press on
Simple paranoia rages inside me
   Surrounded by familiar strangers I've never been so alone
Shall I cut them free?
Sever their needy branches,
that gently throttle the life on which they feed
I rest my eyes
My guard falls
Accusations fly
   ...hope is a bankrupt emotion in the land of thieves

eyes of sovereignty

I feel your presence inside
Your emotions turn to me
My thoughts run wild
I know you're out there
Wandering the land
Confusion run rampant
Questions in hand
My heart beats with rapture
I hope that you know
I still think about you
Wherever I go
Every time you think of me
I see your face so clear
Your heavy heart is wracked with pain
Your eyes are filled with tears
The battle behind that gentle face
Much for you to bear
You hide all your pain
Away from those who care
Erect all the walls
Seal up the doors
Blackout the windows
Extinguish all ties
Plot a new course on the road to my dreams
Stamp out the weaklings
Let them all see
The creation they worshiped was only a man
His ashes remain

Nothings left of their plans
Mishandled and shackled to selfish desire
Drained of his life blood
Vanquished by fire

The Guardian

I grasp the wall curiously,
probing fingers search for answers,
harsh coarseness my welcome companion.
A great barrier,
surrounding a vast lake
where all my fears could be stowed.
The wall stands as a valiant soldier,
beaten by the elements
that erode the foundation of my sanity.
My newfound strength,
spawn of its shadow,
shoulders the wicked winds.
The wall travels on
ending just beyond the line of my sight
and the scope of my imagination.
It never strays from its watery temptress.
Loyalty transcends the stone backbone.
I walk slowly,
dragging my hand
over its worn stories, lost loves, senseless graffiti.
Cold sobriety wracks my body.
I break into a run,
rocketing to the end.
I have to find the riches
near the end of this great,
fossilized rainbow,
that enable this place
to rip the fear from my heart.

Reassurance

Haven't I told you you're special

Worth a thousand words of praise

Haven't I called to say I love you

On those long and lonely days

Rest your head on my shoulder

Let me dry those windswept eyes

Call on me for confidence

Look for bluer skies

Never sell out for fame and fortune

Wealth and happiness aren't one and the same

Listen to a voice that sings of rapture

Follow the dream that calls you by name.

A Cure for Writer's Block

I wrote about a gorgeous lake,
mirrored with trees and sky.
He curled up his nasty lips
and asked what kind of poet was I?

I brushed myself off and stood to my feet,
knowing for sure I had been beaten.
Then once again, I picked up my pen,
I'd coin a new phrase to defeat him.

I conjured up a castle grand,
surrounded by hills of green.
Once again, he laughed at my plan,
with insults so threatening and mean.

"What nonsense," he said, "to make up those places,
Silly, my dear to give life to blank faces.
Time should be spent on practical matters,
Not wagging your tongue with meaningless chatter."

Never before had she heard so much drivel.
No matter her method his thoughts would unravel.
An artist must sculpt, must mold and create.
Always make gold of what's left on your plate.

With one last ditch effort she clinched her eyes shut,
Envisioning a beastie whose thirst was for blood.
Nine feet tall and in search of a meal,
Eyes blazing crimson and claws of steel.

One whack of its talons could rip one to shreds,
Biting and chewing and gnawing their head.
The next thing she knew the air had gone quiet,
Where was her critic to laugh, squawk and riot

Something on the ground caught her wandering stare,
Something peculiar. Something in pairs.
Where once he had stood voicing his critique,
were two matching sneakers, with two matching feet.

So remember dear children, when others create,
Be kind and listen or suffer the fate.
Of one bitter buddy who thought poetry silly
And ended up fodder in a monster's, hungry belly.

Fantasy

She places her faded, red scarf upon the mantle. She knows only one emotion, but can't tell you what that is. A cloud of confusion is her only companion in this new darkness. Hope. The last thing anyone expects to see in her world. They can see the face. The contorted smile. The lines of her forehead tell a story of unfathomable loss. There are questions born of desperate curiosity, no one dares to ask. A man standing across the room speaks inaudibly into a silver sliver of a cell phone. His voice the caliber of angel speak. His lips form words audible miles away. A crowd gathers outside, below the shattered pieces of broken window, just out of sight of the inhabitants of the room. Whispered murmurs of how and why can be felt as well as heard, by those waiting above.

The woman's first movements are stiff and deliberate; a resurrected corpse. The man quietly lowers the phone. Their eyes never meet. She stands cautiously. He adjusts his position, moving closer, thinking... Her calm, uplifted hand of surrender proves his thought true. Graciously, she accepts the assistance. Releasing herself from his grasp, she closes the distance between her seat and the weathered balcony. As she moves, her motion gains the fluidity she lacked upon first rising.

She reaches for the railing. Not to steady herself, but in anticipation of the view below. The sky seeps with blue intensity. The thick air settles like water on her pallid skin. He follows behind, careful not to move too close and never to set foot on the area overhanging the street. The residual shards dissolve into powder under her metered footfalls. In the room, the abandoned scarf dances wildly on the invisible thermals of the fire in the hearth, its fibers coerced to ignite by the persuasive nature of the flames. As it smolders, thick smoke permeates the room. She turns, finally catching a glimpse of what the man is wearing. His leather jacket, glows strangely in the afternoon sun. His eyes bear no resemblance to any she has seen before. Skillfully, she remains poised on the terrace, shifting her gaze to the heavens and buildings nearby. The metallic messenger springs to life in the man's pocket; a momentary distraction. A breeze works its way around her and coaxes the crimson sash from its precarious perch, lifting it skyward only but a moment, before it cascades effortlessly off the mantle, mirroring the woman as she quietly begins her own descent.

The crowd falls silent.

Midwater Madness

What's he doing down there?

   Feeding.

Feeding?

   Fighting demons. Combating fear. Consuming energy. The essence
of foreign power sources in his life

How long can he stay down there?

   As long as it takes.

Suspended in the matrix of his fear,

he floats alone,

mid-water,

halfway between Heaven and Hell.

The direction either of which he's unsure.

Facing down an enemy that hunts with despair and distraction.

Ammunition supplied by the mind of the hunted.

He visits the battlefield this time to stare down the beast,

find a way to deactivate self inflicted paralysis.

Survival flashes scan the surface of his brain;

solar flares escaping the incestuous gravity of their master.

Cold chills sink their daggers beneath the artificial skin.

A registry of pain.

A neural override.

The mission continues.

A mental detonation sequence begins.

He embraces the biological explosive,

as frantic ticking resounds in his ears.

A proud heart beats within him.

The surrounding water electrifies.

Opposing forces unleash a maelstrom of torturous emotion.

He absorbs a volatile mixture of truth and reason,

the antidote for the virus embedded in his being.

Eyes closed, he accepts that life is radically changing.

Seconds begin their final aerobic descent.

Doubt loosens the grip on its former slave.

Spiritual fire consumes the fiction,

eradicating mental errors.

One more second to purity.

New circuitry pulses to life.

An explosion splinters the mortal casing.

Charred pieces slip eerily into the depths.

His true essence screams toward the surface.

 ...a new breed of defender rises from the darkness.

Redemption

No one is so cryptic
As to hold temptation in
Somewhere in the mystery
A leak gives way to sin

Trivial seduction
A lure to catch the beast
Secrets buried rising
And savored like a feast

Sinking in the turmoil
Our vision blurred we miss
The only wall of solace
falls deep in the abyss

For each and every trial
Is seen by those we love
We do not know we're showing
Our heart has had enough

Truth be told, stories emerge
To cleanse us from the lies
Silent vows are lifted
The screen falls from our eyes

Judgment is a farce my child
A hurdle we all must face
Only when we bare our souls
Will sorrow give way to grace

Reminisce

The room grows dark as the light sinks below high, banked windows. Must permeates the warm, stagnate air. An evening breeze sifts casually under an open pane. The heat of the day bakes the inner walls, resurrecting hidden memories. The pungent odor of a gentleman's cigar mingled with the elegant perfume of the lady of the house. A smell of profane age persists over these, one where death is looked upon as the benchmark of life. A fragrance that reminds one of the happy thoughts left behind as one passes from this world. Not one of sadness, but a scent that recollects the stories and faces these walls have seen. Regal wallpaper buckles slightly; wrinkles etched in the profile of a distinguished nobleman. The floorboards maintain their futile defense against relentless termites, mercilessly gnawing away at their history. The house continues its timeless conversation with the harsh winds. A soft, audible moan wanders the hallways.

Samson's Song

Deep inside my heart there's a place that you must go
Rooms so full of sunlight, but no true doors or windows
This place bears no power and holds no mystical lore
It's simply a place, where all of my memories are stored

I go there each night when there's no one around
It's there that I know inner peace can be found
There are pictures, and papers and dusty, old books
Trinkets and bobbles in each little nook

The room I most love when visiting this place
Is one filled with loved ones long since passed away
Each precious soul that touched part of my life
Gone not forgotten as I travel through time

Everyone here has captured my heart
Present are those who helped play a part
By shaping the person I am today
Bodies may go, but memories remain

Hibernation

I rest on the verge of great precipice
A plateau that transcends my existence
rising out of the mists of nowhere.
Its galvanized edges limited only by my Creator.
Spiritual skid marks crisscross my soul
Each moment an adventure begins
Another unexpectedly ends
In a lesson
Along the journey
Archaic thought patterns lie as abandoned interstates to the
ghost towns of my past
New highways are forged
Scouting parties dispatched
Doubt is in abundant supply
The expeditions persist
Life lurches forward
I stumble through a primordial haze
Page twelve of the evening news is being read by the world
As I unwrap the morning edition from weeks past
The wanton pulse of life
Entices me with questions
Answers are nourished by roots of deception.
Have I missed the joint gathering of the minds?
Are the modern intellectuals beyond the reach of my
knowledge?
Worldly opportunities pass me by
I feign the excuse that my dreams are bigger than theirs

I am called to do more than the box to which I've been relegated
Yet I sit,
quietly watching as the uniquely random share the spoils
at the end of my rainbow.

Who do you trust?

Who do you trust?
Once upon a time it was everyone
Life got a little harder
People became harsher
The percentage slowly faded
'Older and Wiser' is the excuse adults use
Passing on their bankrupt, emotional DNA
Breeding paranoia in delicate, little minds
So ask me today
Who do you trust?
No one
I might be prompted to say
Trust is a facade
I lie to protect myself
Ultimately everyone lies
To their friends.
husbands
wives
family
Sick minds incubate white, hot lies
Dormant they lie
Who can I trust?
Mom lied to protect Dad
Dad lied to protect me
And somewhere in the darkness the baby died
   A little white lie on the tip of the tongue
   Turns black the heart that is on the run

Cutting the Cord

I won't hold you against your will
We do so many things in the name of guilt
And in light of life's "have to's"
I grant you freedom
Political asylum from the bipolar, warring parties inside my
head
An unlocking of your caged soul
For who would I be
If I ran free
Yet planted my feet on the foundations of your liberty
Would I be able to breathe
Without the fear of your subtle retaliation
My life was created to help others
I long to set fire to the prison walls that hold you fast
Banish the chains
Which bind you with guilt
Each one in its own time
A gradual release of power
If I were to let it all loose at once
Life as you know it would crumble
You'd become lost in the rubble
So I set you free on the path
    to wash away the evil holding your dreams at bay
Free to a place you don't believe in yet
Nor want to be
Go and see

Severance

For every turn to evil
There is a dissociation of flesh from the soul
A severance from reality
Flesh leads us away
From the paths we are meant to travel
We are enticed on a journey of pleasures
A jaunt through the land of the lost
Temptations pierce the delicate structure of our knowledge
Leaving the mental fabric in ruins
Resting on the edge of my dreams
My soul struggles for sanity
A foothold on sacred ground
A priceless gift

Back Porch Recollections

Perforations in the fabric of time
allow the days to be ripped from my grasp.
Suddenly, the predictable
is replaced by a black and sullen maybe.
Fears I never knew,
lies I never told,
come to light in the shadows.
Every day is a blessing.
Gratitude abounds.
Wishes give way to sorrow.
Never before have I been so alone.
Trudging along as I wander back home.
I've been there.
I've visited.
I've never been back.
Other adventures,
something always lacked.
Whereas before one goal o'er the coals roasted,
Now like a shepherd,
I tend three,
though not boasting.
Spiritual, Mental, Physical and such,
Never before have I asked for so much.
A move of the spirit.
A wrinkle in time.
A chance event in earth tones,
will make them all mine.
I simply must work,

must achieve,
I must pray.
Then I'll awaken
and triumphantly say.
The bills are all paid,
the Orcas are here.
I can swim for miles,
And I've conquered my fears

Remembrance

I knew death was imminent. I could feel it condensing from the heavy air. I heard the approach of foreign soldiers. I was there when the lone man failed to cross the line drawn in the sand. It was evident that none of us knew what we were doing. More than a sense of duty, I felt a longing for the future of this great land. A desire to press onward no matter what lay beyond the walls of this lone gravesite. My own personal fight was magnified in the spirit of the men gathered here. Hopelessness, a resounding whisper on the wind, was tempered with a dream that were our lives lost, it would not be in vain. Whatever lay on the other side of these hallowed walls, regardless of victory or defeat, would never crush the valiant cry of freedom for all men. No man knows the strength of the fight left in him until he is faced with his own mortality. It is said that our lives are nothing more than a vapor, a formless wisp of smoke on the horizon of mortal existence. Where there is smoke, the fire of indignation and resilience will rise. As I fight against an army of infinite hostility, backed by harsh motives. I have great hope that as my body releases the living force that drives it forward. Others will stand in this place where we once fought bravely. They'll hear the tales of our timeless story. The flames of freedom will ignite in their lives as well. Moved to tears they will remember a cry that permeates the fabric of time. My spirit will live on, the battle will rage. Resolution will come. New ground will be claimed. The memories of our demise in the face of freedom will remain forever etched in the hearts of those who hear our names and sense our spirit that hangs over this place.

I stood a few rows back as Santa Ana's men clumsily

scaled the walls. We stood in awe as our stand for freedom transformed our strong fortress into a makeshift tomb. The enemy descended our side of the wall. Their very footfalls transformed the sacred earth beneath to a burial ground.

My eyes were fixed towards the rising cacophony of soldiers, stampeding horses and vigilant humanity. My grip gradually tightened on my weapon. I could feel my faith transferring from my God to the shiny, metal savior nestled in my hands. The first man I brought down restored an ample bit of sanity. He fell, only feet from my position. I flinched as his tyrannous gaze dissolved into the realization that death was but one labored breath away. I reloaded my weapon as other men took up the fight, blasting more of the opposition, invading our fort and my sense of peace. Glancing up from my gun, I took aim at another red-coated furor. The flow of liquid humanity continued to ascend the north corner. It was impossible to maintain my focus as the horizon bloomed with an endless red tide. They were coming at a rate none of us could have imagined. I began to notice my own fallen colors amongst the corpses of the invaders. My eyes raced across the faces in a mindless panic, neither registering nor recognizing my fallen comrades. I snapped back long enough to fire off a second shot as my body was launched backwards into the dirt. I closed my eyes as my flight ended. I sensed a pain, pulsating below my left eyelid. My vision was blurred slightly as I opened the right and reluctantly the left. The sky above shown brightly, the richest blue my mind had ever encountered. I raised my hand to locate the source of my pain. Moisture erupted onto my fingertips in hot rhythmic bursts. Before my fingers even touched my lips, the molten iron incense of my own life force, tinged the air around me. I mouthed a silent prayer before my attacker made his way to my side. Standing over me, a great hunter examining the state of his kill. I closed my eyes once again, negotiating a silent merger with a familiar friend. My metal savior had forsaken me. As I loosened my grip on the stalk, I pulled my hands close to my chest and realigned my faith to its proper position. I heard the shot fire, as if miles away. Pitch black returned. Only this time regaining my vision entailed more than simply lifting an eyelid. All I knew was, the pain was gone. They left me for dead. The swirl of clouds and gun smoke overhead were part of the dream my last few moments on earth had become. Paralysis was my only comfort. No more movement would summon the Mexican predators. I contemplated my life, my death and the stories they would tell of our misfortune; our stand against evil. I was comforted by my efforts and my unyielding stance as acidic bouts of fear swelled within my throat. The mental bullets I dodged, hammered every ounce of resolve I had left. The enemy fire that ended my life came almost as a relief. It quelled the fear. I embraced the peaceful darkness and focused my face towards heaven.

Demise in the Face of Freedom

Death was imminent.
I could feel it condensing from the heavy air
I heard the approach of foreign soldiers
When the lone man failed to cross the line drawn in the sand
I was there
None of us knew what we were doing
More than a sense of duty
There was a longing for the future of this great land
A desire to press on no matter what lay beyond the walls of this
lone gravesite
My own personal fight was magnified in the spirit of the other
men gathered here
Hopelessness, a resounding whisper on the wind
Tempered with a dream that our lives would not be lost in vain
Whatever lay on the other side of these hallowed walls
Victory or defeat
It would never crush the valiant cry of freedom for all men
No man knows the strength of the fight left in him
Until he is faced with his own mortality
Our lives are nothing more than a vapor
A formless wisp of smoke on the mortal horizon
Where there is smoke
The fire of indignation and resilience exist as well
As I fight against an army of infinite hostility
Backed by harsh motives.
I have great hope
As my body releases the living force that drives it forward
Others will stand in this place where we once fought bravely

They'll hear the tales of our timeless story
And the flames of freedom will ignite in their lives as well
Moved to tears they will remember
A cry that permeates the fabric of time
My spirit will live on
Battle will rage once again
Resolution will come
New ground will be claimed
And the memories of our demise in the face of freedom
Will remain forever etched in the hearts of those who hear our names
And sense our indomitable spirit that hangs over this place

Never Love Again

And through the rain
I see the blindings of my fate on the horizon,
a sun drenched laser,
cutting into the base of all that I stand for.
I see the paths of my past,
rivers of deceit I have cried.
I see no way out of this passionless life,
where anything has the capacity
to stimulate the nerve endings of demon perversion in my
mind.
No end to the terror of my ways.
I am worried,
I will die,
never having felt the love for a woman in my heart.
If this is so,
Can I go on?
The best way to defeat an opponent
is not to cast him down with fists of rage,
but rather
to issue unto him
the life that was dealt to me.

Sunrise Confessions
January 7, 1997

Having not lived your life,

How could I know your pain?

See the wounds you've sustained.

Other than knowing your heart has been crushed;

A ritual that repeats with the sunrise,

A terror committed not by an enemy,

You are the only suspect in this senseless crime.

You interpret other's visions for your life,

Slaying yourself on a rancid altar of pity,

Their deadliest weapon is an aptly placed suggestion.

Your heart melts.

All I am is antifreeze for your soul.

Your heart can't be reached.

They won't touch the core of your being.

It's the only security that each morning when you awake,

Together we pick up the pieces,

Slipping each tiny fragment back into place.

We smile.

Thank God that we found one another,

before the world outside convinced us

that there was no hope left.

For our love,

our kind.

The Passion of Regret

The party of life is soon ended for the young
when they see the fruits of their labor,
sewn in the sand before them.
They can no longer progress as children,
but must function as adults who possess
a new realism about life.
If I had known the outcome,
there are things I'd have never done.
Those days are over.
I mourn the remembrance of ancient, emotional roller
coasters.
Yet I relish the last, deep breaths of their faded euphoria.
No longer will I dwell on the excavation of ghostly graves
in my mind.
I must put my past to rest;
A collection of foreign memories from a life I once led.
My heart is no longer reflected in their seductive sheen.
I choose now to finish the remaining years of my life,
walking in the way I once thought impossible,
but desperately wanted to believe.
I must bury the dead.
My future is born anew.

Walls

March 14, 1996

To the walls of the world,
I give my color.
I paint them in an array of light,
that gives substance to my being.
The walls are there not for me,
but for the basic success of life around us.
We see them as barriers,
obstacles to be vanquished.
To overcome is magnificent.
Break down the walls.
Paint them with every hue of your moral fiber.
Sew the seeds that one day your children will reap.
Live life!
So when it is over,
you may say that life has been good.
Words of wisdom to live by.
Adopt a world unlike your own.
Make it worth your while.
Delve not into sin and immorality.
Invest your time in the fruits of the spirit.
And you shall truly live.
Love,
a weapon against all that dares harm you.
When you truly care for the unfortunate of the earth,
thou art truly a hero.
All will look up to you.

You in turn should look up to God.
Pray for the wisdom he gives so many.
God is love.
And IF we are with God,
Then we are truly loved.

Ship Lights

Lights shine from a place just beyond my reach.
You can sense their energy,
as it travels across the darkness,
on its journey to my soul.
Nothing more than ship lights on the ocean.
One by one they unite,
looking as a barrier that provides a sense of security.
I wonder if my energy is strong enough to be felt by them.
Do they sense my fear at not being heard?
Surely they do.
For as they sparkle,
from one realm of brightness to the next,
a single voice echoes in my mind.
And I feel their pain.

Dual Personality

He creeps into the cupboard
To find a crust of bread

It slips into the crevice
The folds inside your head

He finds a piece of cracker
A morsel he can chew

It digs a little deeper
To find what makes you, you

First he nibbles then he munches
To savor this tiny feast

Reaching near the center
A curious little beast

His meal quite gone, but hungry
Still he crouches low to see

If the tunnel he's been digging
Is enough to harvest me

Save the Wounded Souls

Candidly they would sit by themselves
Outcast and alone
On occasion angels sifted down love from heaven
Every now and then
Making life bearable
They knew they must rid themselves of their beasts
Thoughts forever drifted
Straying from the Lord.
Not one of them knew that the error of ways
Would lead them to an untimely death
Some say they had choices
How to die
How to live
But was it really living?
These choices were governed by invisible rules
Unseen
like the boundary between day and night
Silent
as the blood coursing through a vein

The Lake

There was a wall surrounding the lake
made of stone
as those of old in England
walls abundant in the days of Robin Hood

The sun was barely shining
it had no apparent bearing
it wasn't cold
yet a chill was in the air

The lake was peaceful
I felt at peace with myself
even though I'd had a bad day
that lake and that wall together were my healing forces

I can't get over the feeling that being there gave me

Fraternal Disorder

As the movie ended
I saw it creeping towards me in the dark
Fear materialized
Flavoring my saliva
Paralyzed by the form coming my way
Light gave way to a realization
The creature before me
Nothing more than a mirror of my past.
How many times
With my eyes locked on target
Had I aimed for the heart
And landed in the crotch
Setting my sights on anything with the capacity to soothe
And now this innocent one
His movements cloaked darkness
Shuffled closer
Fleshy intentions
Kinetic imaginations
Feeding the hunger that raged inside him
He crouched before me
Resting near my feet
The boldness in his gate faded
Expressive eyes glazed
Darting nervously around the room
Searching for a reason that existed seconds before
Surveying the safety of this dark chamber
Words came in whispers

I know our paths are similar
Once again the gaze moved
Turning downward
I know you know who I am
Suddenly fear morphed into anger
My own inner demons released
Lashing out
I protect myself with hostile, verbal distractions
Once control is regained
I send the beast back to its lair
Hoping that if it ever resurfaces
My heart will be a safe distance away

Do You Love Me

Do you love Me?
Enough to give up your will and choose mine?
To walk with Me
Every single moment
Of every single day
Do you love Me?
Does the fact that I know your every thought and still cherish
you mean something to you?
Does the fact that I have
    felt your pain
        and endured greater struggles,
make you love Me even more?
Do you love Me on the days when you wake up
and fear courses through your veins like the blood that ran
down My brow on the cross?
Do you love Me?
Enough to stand watch as I kneel in the garden to pray
Do you love Me?
Though you don't understand My methods or My ways
I hope so
No matter how many lashes came to greet My body that fateful
night
I saw your shining face
I saw the whip in the hand of the woman whose life I would
gladly save
I saw the fear tempered with anger on the face of the last man
to drive the stake through My wrist
I felt

the tears behind the emotion
the despair behind the guilt
I felt them all
Bore them all
Became them for a season
I would do it all again
So I ask you now
Not out of necessity
But out of sheer desire
Do you love Me?
Do you love Me enough to share the pain masked by the
problems of this world?
Do you love Me enough to lay aside your emotional weapons
and walk toward Me?
I long for nothing more than to hold you in My arms whether
you love Me or not
To share with you My plan for your life
Heal your wounds
Right the wrongs
Do you love Me?
Are the scars in your life there because of your efforts to sustain
them?
My scars are proof of nothing more than the fact that I love you.
I was there when you sought comfort in the arms of another
man
I held you both as you marinated in the duality of your pain
I walked along with you
I called your name

It was My eyes you searched for
as you frantically scanned the crowd that night
When I met your gaze you quickly looked away
It was My arms that held you when you sobbed inner tears so great
that to birth them would have brought about unparalleled insanity.
I lifted you up when you had trouble seeing over the clouds
I made it possible that your every wish
Every desire could be fulfilled
One night
As I made the decision to give up My will
Combat the fear welling up inside Me
With great tears of blood falling from My eyes
I gave up my own desires in this world
My very life was laid before you
Giving you the opportunity to live your life
So I ask you
With great anticipation
And a heart that rejoices each time a lost soul calls My name
from the darkness
Do you love Me?

Alias

March 11, 2004

I am compromised O God by the apple of my eye.
Because of my fear of rejection and loneliness,
My decisions are not of a Holy nature.
I see with my flesh.
My mind lulls my spiritual side to sleep.
I pursue treasure that can never be uncovered.
The wealth I seek is not of eternal threads.
I am blinded by desire and falsified dreams.
I long to be wanted, loved and desired,
not for my love of You,
but simply for the person I am.
I long to be someone else,
somewhere else.
It is a desire sewn of the flesh.
I must lay it down and
cause my vision to be restored and refocused to God's plan.

Anger (Under New) Management

The crash sounded so near
I whipped my head around to pinpoint the direction
Seeing nothing
I returned to my prior gaze
Then it hit me
A feeling of inner turmoil
The crash had come from inside my head
I have heard people say
"Then my world came crashing down"
I was unaware that it could be heard
In the midst of it
I realized
It could be felt as well
I had always had a sense of who I was
Now it felt as if the plateau I'd been resting on had collapsed
underneath me
My bearing was off
One emotion could be felt with more clarity than the rest
Anger
My head hurt at the familiarity of it
I had been angry before
The tide was rising within me
I could feel my skin redden
Heat radiated all around me
Giving life to my rosy glow
Slumber
My only escape
A ritualistic, death nap was the only drug capable of purging

this unwelcome visitor

The crash had echoed through my cells

My heart beat rhythmically with the pulsating waves of rage in
my head

A call to arms reverberated through my mind

Don't let the sun set on your wrath

As sleep came

I laughed in the face of madness

Then fought with my demons all night long

Upon waking in the morning

Rage awaited me in its many forms

   A thief, poised and ready to steal my joy

      An emotional hangover, remembrance of my failures

        Regret and her many sisters

        Ravenous concubines of my thoughts

In Silence Comes My Energy

August 1, 1999

In Silence comes my energy
I listen and observe
Resting my emotions
I draw on Mother Earth

Through fear I've found submission
Embraced a tattered heart
Crouching in the darkness
I wait to act my part

Each day my soul grows stronger
My body heals with time
Vision is returning
Memories echo the crime

In battle lies my passion
A healing force sublime
Season of hibernation
Then I will rise divine

Nightfall welcomes morning
Sleep is long since past
Victory is fleeting
Each breath may be your last

In silence comes my energy
Armor clad I rise
A world cries out for justice
Dissension floods the skies

Passing Through

I walk on shaky ground
My steps always fall
One after the other
I never stopped pursuing my goal
I know not where I am going
I press on
I know not what lies ahead
My eyesight has faded
Instinct drives me on
Fear never holds me back
When I am tired
Rest will come
Dreams remind me of all I have done
The journey that lies ahead
Though my body grows weak
My spirit lives on
In the hearts of those who knew me
Death was just another stop on this eternal tour
I lived a long life
I touched many
They will forever have the image of me
Emblazoned in their hearts and minds
This time rest came suddenly
I can see the light again
No shadows cloud my view
Boundaries that once held me fast are broken
Shattered remains lay under my feet
I run with a renewed passion

Freedom comes in strange packages
There will be no more stillness for me
I've rested long enough
Time is a constant
Not a luxury in this place

Shattered

August 29, 2004

In the end it was my heart that broke the silence
The voice in my head stood as a quiet sentinel
Something snapped
No longer able to stand
Rigid and composed
A valiant warrior
Pretending that offenses never penetrated the inner walls
Futile resilience was laid to rest
The disarmament of my soul began
The deep azure pools of my eyes breached their borders
Every spoken word
An assault capable of leading me down rage road
Dark passions
Burned hotter and brighter than any star in the heavens
Anger surfaced that can only be quenched as the soul it devours
erupts into flames
My heart led the resistance
The members of my body joined rank
One by one they surrendered to the darkness
Leaving my heart to carry on a silent facade it was never meant
to sustain
In time it shattered under the pressure
The chaotic bitterness being held at bay
Burst forth
Flowing violently
Consuming every Innocent in its path

Blind Ambition

December 26, 2002

You'll have to forgive me.

I saw our love as a chance to escape.

To be free from a lifetime of painful, indelible memories.

When I let my heart go,

I imprisoned your soul.

In a single moment,

I orchestrated our past, present and future,

as if we had already lived them.

I needed something in my life to go as planned.

    Your flesh,

        A necessity.

    Your opinion,

        Negligible.

I loved the thought of settling down,

more than I loved the thought of you.

My heart cried out for normal,

long before my lips ever whispered your name.

I loved the safety of lying next to you,

forever safe and loved in your arms.

My sanity preserved.

I loved the thought of always having someone around,

a kindred spirit at my disposal.

As I close the storybook fantasy I have written for your life,

I loathe the thought of missing you.

It would imply my feelings ran deeper than I care to admit.

I wasn't as cold and calculating as I presumed.

In the well thought out process of not taking a risk,

emotions controlled my footfalls one second longer than my
logic.
I realize now,
I am learning to appreciate you, too late.
I am sorry.
You were a sacrifice on the altar of my selfish desires.
In the end,
my needs were far too great for anyone to meet.
In the interest of mending my wounds,
I casually devoured an innocent heart
and simply forgot...
to love you.

Release

April 30, 2003

In the stillness of my heart
I can feel His breathing
His decision to let each and every beat fall as planned
I can feel the pulse of His laughter
As I discover the hidden blessings He has for me
I can sense His approval
I give Him the glory for my blessings.
I lean in
Feel the warmth of His presence
Stronger than any man that has ever held me
More beautiful than any companion I have ever loved
His love for me cost Him everything
He gave it to me freely
He paid my bills in full
And then handed me the keys
So that one day I could hand them back to Him.
It took a long time to release the love He deemed unnatural
It felt so true
Incubated in lies
Little by little the truth battled to rise to the surface
One day I leapt into a new world through faith
As the clouds faded from my view
I felt Him
Waiting there
Ready to show me love that would nurture my dreams
And heal my wounds

First Love

I see your eyes shining upon me
They pull me close
Welcome me to the meeting of our souls
You touch my hand
I am transported
Where dreams line up on an ancient cliff
Taking flight into an open sunset
I see your heart as it melds with mine
I know your only will is mine
I love you
And feel the need to touch you
Know where you began
So that I may see
How my life began also

Thanks Mom

Don't worry bout me I'll be fine
You've taught me all you know
I hold it close inside my heart
My mind makes sure it's used
You taught me all there is to right and wrong
How to choose the path and not to stray
How to survive in this world every day
I think of you
How my life was lucky enough
To radiate outward from your mind filled with knowledge
Your life filled with hard labor
And a heart that beats with love

Free

Grasp the tree limb
Ponder crossing the creek
Fish jump at a distance
Breaking out of their watery world
For a glimpse of yours
Shoes on the bank
Toes kick at the frigid water
Mud loosening
Feet slipping
Wild flailing
Ominous splash
Heart pounding
Frantic searching for a hold on anything
Creatures scurrying
Hesitant relaxing
Going under
Refreshing breezes

The Search

Unlike the earth where molten rock boils and churns
My core has long since cooled
All motion has ceased
My window of opportunity has closed
I know
As the last drop of anesthetic soaks into my soul
I long for a light that shines from within
Different than the cold, flickering illumination
That dances across my face and withers away
Eventually
I am left to combat the madness of the dark corners of my mind
Alone...still.

Mental Gymnastics

I feel the need to fall in love.
I feel the need to pursue my dreams.
I feel the need to be free.
I feel a sense of entrapment.
I need a way out of this life in order to find the one I really want
to live.
I want to be famous.
I want to be able to sing like Whitney Houston.
I want to be near a true friend.
I want a break to live my dreams.
I want to be me.
I want to be different.
Fulfilled by my desires.
Loving who I am when I am that person.

Revenge

Call me from the clouds
If you are prepared to deal with me
I am stronger now
I could eliminate your worries
By killing you
Call me out of the sky
Suffer the wrath of God
For He has put me there
To commune with Him
Listen to the cries of those you torture
Call me from the dead
To tell the secrets of fate
I have seen the way you die
I am jaded to your whimpering
Killing you now is the answer
So the ones you hurt may never feel agony
But revel in your demise
I am against you
Your vial prophecies come true
I live to see your life flow
Spilled like a river overflowing sacred banks
I will drink of your essence as your lifeless corpse gives
unselfishly
And the maggots
As they drain the last glint of light from your immortal soul
Sweet music to my ears

Freeze Warning

December 2002

Winter
The most devastating time of the year
Earth
Mysteriously stripped of its brilliance
The air
Once refreshing and calm
Laps viciously at the core of your being
To quench the life within
Winter
A time when change occurred with greater frequency
The color of life around me faded
Along with my sense of hope
Winter was a time when
   Relationships had ended
      Romantic notions were remembered
         Loneliness perforated the last shred of happiness
Despair
Though a foreigner in warmer climes
Hacked away at my sanity
When the first leaf began to turn
The chill that settled into my bones
Ransacked my mind
Stealing my dreams from sight

Brotherly Love

If you are like me
Somewhere in the darkness
You hear whispers that call you by name
Like an old friend
Quietly they call
Delicately they slit your throat
Letting your moral lifeblood slip away
I know you are scared
Fear beats louder in your chest than your own heartbeat
Afraid of failure
So much so that you program it into your every day
In hopes that if you do not succeed
You will be covered
All bets are off
No one expects anything from you anyway
The faith to move mountains
Beyond your grasp
Purpose defeated in your own mind

Lost Child

June 13, 2006

There is great pain lurking there that no one will ever see
Poised
Perched behind my eyelids
Wedged between tears and emotion
Like a rabid dog
I fight daily to keep it back
I hold it at bay
Keep it from affecting my life
To release it would be to admit failure
Embrace my own humanity
Allow weakness to play on the movie screen I display for all the world to see
I don't want them in here
With their dime store therapy evaluation of what is best for me
I have enough garbage rumbling around inside my head
Without them bringing order to the metered chaos
That governs my daily migration between fear and aggression
The doorway for me to be reached has long since closed
Slammed shut. Nailed. Sealed forever
Like the lid of a coffin
I rest in the comfortable slumber of eternal panic
Where were they when I needed them?
Wanted them?
When my heart vacationed near the deep end of the dark spectrum

Love has never been anything more than an avenue down which
destruction freely travels
 So here I stand
Knowing the only way you will ever affect my life
Is through the fractured glass of the window through which I
view the world
Why should I trust you?
You wait there
Encased in the same cryptic, humanity as all the others
Pedaling your stale wares
As if you have something new to offer me
My thick skin will never let you see the one thing that matters
The fragrant essence of death that grows round my heart
With each new face that appears and disappears from the
window
You'll never know
Lest you see it
Perceive it
Lest you love me without shame
Through the hardness
The Pain
Unless you stay around long enough to help me find the little
boy lost in exile
Roaming around
Bewildered
In the chaos of my mind

Last Curtain Call

As the applause tapers off
So does the rush of adrenaline.
Until there is nothing left of your legal fix
Save the hangover of reality
The masses
Like a great pride of lions
Cry out to be fed daily
What satisfied them today
Simply will not do tomorrow
Daily you sacrifice your dignity on the altar
No price too great
To hear the roar
Feel the rush
As it generates the chemical your brain craves
Catapulting you higher yet again
If only you could
Maintain it
Sustain it
Capture it
Detain it
One moment longer than yesterday
So addictive
So right.
Eventually,
The warmth of the lights fade
Exchanging stardom for the winter of the soul
You slip into a crevasse of mediocrity
Moonlight fails to illuminate your darkness

Alone you lay in a heap
Scattered debris and ransacked emotions
Memories your only link to a time when you reigned supreme
You stare wantonly across a vast expanse
Once filled with a writhing mass of humanity
Whose sole purpose was to nurse your vanity
Realization creeps in
A seductive, cerebral marauder
Seeking to devour the remaining virtue of your dreams
Truth pierces your soul like a poison dart
Quenching the very life that sustains your glory
Wincing in pain
One final thought ascends from the depths
Before eternal, black night descends upon you

... it's hard to live in a world where people have forgotten you're a star.

House of my Sorrow

I haven't slept in days,
unable to shake the image of you lying there,
motionless in the street.
I wanted desperately to stop,
search for signs of life,
restore broken pieces.
The coldness told me there was nothing I could do.
As my own heart began to dissolve,
I moved on,
leaving you to lie there.
Despair followed me as I walked,
pursuing me with lurid shouts,
purging me of all other emotions.
My eyes aren't heavy any more.
I've long since stopped crying.
Sheer exhaustion has dried the tears from my eyes.
I loved every mention of your name.
Your stories gave me one more reason to wake.
As I strain my ears for any audible sign,
chilling whispers greet me from the grave.
A voice, not yours, speaks of regret.
I haven't eaten in days,
more a chore than a necessity.
Pictures traverse the highways in my head.
I'll never forget your last involuntary pose.
Shoulders slumped.
Legs bent.
Face blank.

A new canvas.

There was no peace there that some find in death.

Only shadows of the past,

drifting aimlessly across the surface in search of a resting place.

My steps are labored and great.

Ordered by God.

I've walked far enough.

I can't see you when I look back.

The image of your death isn't enough

to erase the indelible marks you made on my life.

Sleep eventually visits the house of my sorrow.

With all power to suppress the memory of you, arrested.

Your life begins to play like a silent film, on the backs of my eyelids.

I fall asleep roaming endless hallways,

filled with your laughter.

The Ritual

July 2, 2007

Everything is so clear to me now
As I sit atop my ivory tower
I can see the life going on around me
The champagne flows as easy as the music
Both work to weaken my defenses
A calculated maneuver
No one knows I'm here
Perched high in the darkness
A soft, blue light on the stereo
My only source of illumination
The light within is all but extinguished
I long to connect to one of the faces out there
Has been prom queen
Rich jerk
Fraternity guy
His girlfriend
It doesn't matter to me
The touch of a warm hand
More welcome than
The kiss of this cold steel on my skin
I would never do it
Never just disappear
So I sit in my contrived, emotional fortress
Coaxing the tears from the depths of their hiding places
They won't come on their own
I must lure them outside
Lulling myself into a drunken stupor
My heart grows sadder still

Alcohol numbs my resistance

Lyrics chip away at my resolve

One singular piece of rock

Breaks free from the wall surrounding my heart

Another races to join it

An avalanche of gypsum forms at my feet

Torrents flow from my eyes

Finally allowed permission to feel my pain

Hours pass

I repeat the process weekly

Desperate to find a way into my core

Mediocrity Personified

Key in the door
Nothing new
Nothing out of place
I cringe
Longing for one sliver of adventure
Casual mediocrity is the ruler of my kingdom
Once again
Another little piece of my heart loses hope
Anticipation gives way to despair
Even the thought of generating some excitement
Fails to bring about the elation it once did
Routing checks are performed
Day's events are contemplated
Still
Hope is my ever, elusive companion
Frustration waits patiently in every corner of the room
Fear greets me with wicked familiarity
Anxious thoughts dart about like snowflakes in a raging, mental
blizzard
Best solution
Retreat into bed
Sleep staves off the evil horde for another few hours
Yet even after waking
I keep my eyes closed
Bluff the enemy
Make another feeble attempt at redemption

I Have Seen the Face of God

I have seen the face of God
Looked upon His grace
My eyes grow weak
As the retinas die an untimely death
Bursting as the bright heat of His presence
Stimulates the core of my humanity
My emotions run in fear of being discovered and hanged
As they lie senselessly on the surface of my soul

I have seen the face of God
Has He seen me?
There by the wayside lying in your shame
Every emotion stripped from a now lifeless body
Bankrupt and useless
Crawl away
Regain the strength it takes to continue the flight from His
presence

My Angel

I sat down next to you
Never seeing the tears
I would have chosen another seat
Another opportunity
I might have missed the moment
But just like I am to my own pain
I was blind to yours
Choosing the seat one away from yours
I heard the sobs
Saw the tissue
Sensed the remorse
The drama in my life was laid aside
To investigate yours
Manage your pain
Because mine had somehow eluded me
I sat there
Quiet and still
Frantically exhausting one scheme after another to find a way
to talk to you
Break into the sphere of your misery
Then you opened the door
"Hello."
Why didn't I think of that?
Suddenly
Random became the natural order of things
Confession spilled from your lips
Reassurance flowed from mine
As I spoke I lowered my defenses long enough

to see a lesson mirrored in your pain.

Peace began to trickle in from an unknown source

By our second, chance meeting

I began to destroy the walls myself

Torrential healing poured over the foundation of my heart

I shared my life

You relinquished your guilt

I called you

      My angel

You called me yours

Our shared tears

Set us both free to examine the truth

I will never see you again

Your words

Indelibly etched onto my heart

Prevention

For a thousand future mistakes

Bringing Together of a Few

In the wake of great trials a soul is set free.

Bodies are laid to rest.

So we may remember,

but never again have to look upon their motionless forms.

New bodies are created for free souls.

A small, infant body is the keeper of a free soul.

The soul's domain is precious.

Great care must be taken not to spill the soul from its container.

When souls and bodies unite.

All rejoice and tears of joy flow forth.

The parting of such a coupling always brings sadness.

The tears flow.

Joy has soon since passed.

Death brings all together as in birth.

But as the story of both soul and body unfold,

Who is watching and caring?

Rubble

When the walls grow high enough
It's impossible to see my face
The only glimpses that anyone gets
Are the images I paint on the outside of the walls
It's incredibly draining to hold these walls up
I feel I have untapped energy supplies
To keep the people out
Maintain these walls
Inevitably they find ways inside
Ways I didn't plan
Pathways I never knew existed
Breaches in the armor
Gaping holes I never repaired
Places of weakness
Secret places
But people find them
Infiltrate my emotional fortress
I am forced to build more walls
In the process
Others fall
Until one day no energy remains
To hold the walls up
Keep the invaders at bay
One by one as the walls fall
I willingly let anyone inside
Tears flood my soul
I die a thousand emotional deaths
Lying naked

Vulnerable in the arms of my captor
I find an uneasy comfort in this invasion
I ask myself what might have happened
If I had lowered the walls, instead of allowing their demise
Sorting through the rubble at my feet
I fashion an existence from the random shards of emotional
debris created in the aftermath of destruction
The cycle continues
Construction begins again

Massacred Emotions

I can't see your face any more
Yet somewhere in the darkness
Your words resonate with brutal clarity
Layer after layer
A life unravels before me
I would have never imagined
Tragedy and resilience kept you alive
Tears sporadically flow
Each word bears the weight of a thousand sorrows
My heart sinks in my chest
With each passing moment
I thank God for the life I have led
For preserving you to share your story
As the layers come off
I see the walls go up
The powerlessness of youth is pushed aside
A strong, young man is being directed by the mind of a scared
little boy
I walk through my day wearing your pain
I take it into my heart and my head
In the end
I walked as close to a mile in your shoes as I could
As the conversation is remembered
A thousand thoughts rush over me
A million things I thought I could fix
God called for silence
I chose to trust Him
To love you

And be still
I continued to listen
I stroked your hair and held you tight
I prayed
Man did I pray
Prayer that made no sense to anyone but God
Words interspersed with great sobs as more tears fell
The truth of the matter
I was so sad and angry that words didn't come for a few days
I kept to myself
Trusting that God brought you into my life for a reason
Whether my words were cleansing or inconsequential
I was obedient
I was moved
Blessed to hear a story that few have heard
When you are ready to cry
About the massacred emotions of a little boy
I will be there
A strong shoulder
A mind to listen
An aching heart
Your prayers call down resolution
Christ's body delivers redemption
One way or another
You're covered

Assassin

What I needed
You could have provided with ease
The cost
Nothing more than kindness
A good deed done in the face of trial
But you set your trap
Baited with the things I needed most
Equal parts love and acceptance
Intermingled with toxin-laden, physical desires you so often
forced on others
I willingly climbed inside
Cutting my knees on the shards of discourse
Deceptively planted amongst the stars in your eyes
Before I realized
The door slammed shut
Breaking my spirit in the process
Severing my will to fight
You had me
Who would want me now?
Wasn't this whole thing somehow my fault?
Pain I experienced at your hand
Outweighed my feelings of acceptance
I realized much too late
Love you had to offer
Came at a price, I was no longer willing to pay
Powerless to stop you
I began to drown in waves of regret
No one could protect me now

No one could save me
Who would come to my rescue?
Who would value me as much as you?
Though your love was deceptive
It was greater than any before
Blinding me to reality
Severing my heart
From the truth

Piracy

July 4, 2006

He holds your heart
I hold you now
What I wouldn't give to have what he has
In my head
I have walked this romantic road before
I exhaust my mind
My heart
My riches
Your part is easy
A simple yes
A nod of your head
As I sit
Counting the treasures of another man
I am tempted to try my hand at piracy
Steal what I want
Losing everything I have in the process

Rise and Fall
March 2, 2006

My heart beats
Waves of hopelessness and ambition
Intermingled with a thousand moods
A contradictory escapade
Life's ebb and flow
Fear and courage penetrate the surface
Intermittently
Momentarily
I drift aimlessly amongst ocean waves
No boat
No companions
Watery hands clasp round my neck
Natural forces work to subdue me
Dark water welcomes despair as it floods over me
How much further I can sink
The wind returns
I feel myself being lifted on the crest of a wave
My spirit soars
I look beyond the watery walls framing my existence
Starlight
Unnoticed before
Gleams from above
New air fills my lungs
Catapulting me high above
A contemptuous valley of death
Hope is reborn
Humanity wages war against this new sense of hope
It has only known defeat

Mixed emotions traverse the surface of my heart

The walls are sure to rise again

Yet whispers of freedom emerge

Before I am once again plunged into the depths

Tongues of black liquid lap up what remains of my resolve

I rise and fall on the ocean

At the mercy of the rolling tides

My light is extinguished

Anger replaces all else

Powerless I descend

Game of Chance

January 30, 2007

At some point applause gives way to silence
You're left alone on stage
Facing an empty auditorium
Only memories of that last amazing moment in the spotlight
At some point the silence gives way to time
With its great capacity
To erase good and bad
Cleansing power dissolving away
Fear, laughter, bitterness, pride
Each new day
A cleaner slate than before
At some point time gives way to peace
With its uncanny ability to soften the passage of years
And weaken the heart just enough
So that we can feel amazing again
Peace settles in and quiets the indignant whispers of regret
Blanketing our fears
Allowing us to find solace in the life we lived
Wrong or right
At some point peace gives way to power.
Unbridled knowledge that something great was accomplished
In the few, short years your face appeared in the window of
earth.
At some point power gives way to death
You find yourself back on the stage
Bright lights blazing once again

Your eyes adjust
This last performance
For an audience of one

At some point applause gives way to silence
You're left alone on stage
Somewhere in the stifling quiet
His single voice calls you by name

Decisions

July 7, 2006

We stand as two sentinels
Defending the beliefs that line up behind us
Silently we face one another
Our strengths
Hidden from the other
Sizing each other up
Opinions begin to form
A choice is made
Use one man's weapons
Destroy those of the other
A decision is made
Cancel any effect we could have on the world
Join forces and affect nation after nation
The unthinkable
One warrior having never broken the stare of the other
Lays down all he has and begins to walk
Unarmed toward his opponent
A second decision is made
Strike while the enemy is most vulnerable
Jump ahead to capture his foe
Or in similar fashion
Lay aside knowledge and reason
Embrace a new concept of freedom

The Presence

Sept 8, 2006

Here I stand
Alone at the edge of the Universe
I've forgotten the things that brought me here
Forgotten how I arrived
Though nothing lies before
Everything lies behind
I can't fight the feeling
I've been here before
The universe appears bigger
As if it has expanded under my gaze
The perimeter is now
Out beyond what I remember
Life's hardest challenges have brought me here
Generating this feeling of...in my life
It feels the same
This thick darkness
This utter isolation
Saturated with uncertainty
Each time the world I find comfort in
Fades away
Falling into rubble behind me
I feel IT there with me
The Presence.
The Voice.
The Light in the void.
So I stand there
Accompanied by fear

Bolstered by courage
And He encourages me
To step forward
Expand my borders yet again

Rise Up: A message from a loving Father

I give each of you different talents
Where you are deficient
I am able to fill in the gaps
I made each of you different
In My great army there will be
Generals, nurses, warriors, martyrs
I etched My plan into the framework of hearts
Thwarting the schemes of the enemy
I equipped you with love
See each human factor in the battle
From warriors on both sides of the battle
I cut out a small piece of their heart
Keeping it for myself.
The wise
Remain in the light
Searching My presence for their missing piece
A sense of wholeness they seek
The foolish
Wander endlessly in darkness
Blind to what is missing from their lives.
The search feeds their frustration
Driving them to destruction.
Rise up
My Son
Prepare for the battle.
Rise up
Brave Warrior
Prepare for War

Reluctant Hero

December 3, 2005

Cautious steps forward
A delicate reminder of the boldness that precedes
Untold preparation
Rage felt if only for a day
In dreams our lives are played out
Words spill forth
Granting revelation
Power restored
In peaceful aspiration
A costly journey unfolds
Resistance is met with staunch denial
The years that were melted away
Slowly begin to materialize on the horizon
Blackout of the mind
Submission
Necessary and requested
Lower the fences
Aim for the heart
Fire the weapons of mass destruction
The mass of emotional baggage growing between us
Separates us from our power source.
Without fear I walk toward my goal
Sharing without concern for my sanity
Feeling the weight of a thousand secret hurts melt away
Boldly I speak of painful memories
Dragging the rancid, metered darkness into the light
I watch as one by one
They are consumed by healing illumination

Truth rushes in
A cleansing stream
Washing away inadequacy
Replacing doubts
Dream of a new beginning

Simple Solution

It is time for me
To no longer be in pain
No longer worry about life
The trouble it brings
Time for me
To reap the benefits of the good I have done
Instead of seeing bad things spring forth
From hiding places beyond my reach
I hurt so much for
A lover and a friend
In one body
So my time between them won't be split
I need healing my own mind generates
Once my needs for basic human kindness have been met
I'll move on from this place
Find the solution to every problem
End the whining with death
Move forward
Look back on this part of my life
Appreciate what I have learned
I seek deliverance from a poison mind
As it shuttles toxic thoughts
To hands that can do me harm
Freedom is all I seek

I haven't the price to open the gates
Set myself free
I tread delicately
A prisoner of life
Fear is my exile

The Hero

There's nothing better than launching an all out assault into enemy territory to rescue civilians. You don't get a high like that from a video game. Sure I was afraid, but fear wasn't my motivator. I had a passion for the mission. I believed in what we were doing. I fought for women and children, praying for the day I'd get back to my own wife and little girl. I served alongside good men. No matter what, they had my back. Our mission was simple. Get in. Get the civilians. Get out. And try to dodge a mile-long line of enemy guards hidden throughout the city. I managed to grab a woman and a baby. I flanked the perimeter and at a clearing, broke into a run. The strangest sound in the world is when everything around you goes quiet. One minute you're in the heat of battle, running full tilt bore to the safe zone, the next, you take a rifle shot in the back and your vision begins to fade. Private Anthony Wilson was my cover man. The force of the shot took me out at the knees. I collapsed. When I looked up Wilson was in shock. My eyes locked on his. I mouthed the words; "Take them to the safe zone." He didn't hear me. He was already in shock. He panicked. He fired off 50 rounds back into the city, dropped his weapon, turned and ran. The last thing I saw was the back of his fatigues. He left us. He just...left us. That's what happened that day. It was a Tuesday. The sky was an odd shade of red. And now I'm here, bathed in white light... in these clothes. That only means one thing to a soldier. I wasn't afraid of dying, but to be left like a common thief to rot in the jungle. I won't get to see my little girl grow up or take her first steps. Or...kiss away my wife's tears when she hears the news of my death. They'll call me a hero. I died giving my life for others. I simply did what was asked of me. I'd do it again. If that makes me a hero, sobeit.

Notes

Black Waters was written as a result of the things I learned about the ocean when I was learning to SCUBA dive. I never knew that the color red disappears first and that blue is the last color to fade. I used this new fact to describe my early struggles with homosexuality and the odd attractions I was having to guys. I never wanted to be gay. I never asked for the feelings. The knowledge that I might be gay led me to out and out moments of hopelessness. This is one of many poems I wrote based on the hopelessness I felt.

Missing You: I wrote this poem many years after the guy I dated the longest broke up with me. At one point I knew he was the person I was going to be with for the rest of my life. Then he was out of my life in an instant. I was lonely and confused. He broke up with me. I was a Christian and he was an Atheist. Not a great match, but it was more about the intimacy for me. I spent a year of my life with this guy. Christians could debate all they want about whether or not our relationship was an abomination to God. It didn't change the fact that the love we felt was real. Our life and times were not going to be forgotten easily. I was battling between my gay life and where God was ultimately leading me. I was very alone at the time as well. I had gone from being very sexually active and intimate with someone to being alone and bitter. This poem was my true confession of the feelings that still lingered and the reality that he was out of my life forever.

Night Pal: This poem has two distinct origins. I grew up very lonely. I was a loner, who was bullied, because I wasn't the most masculine of boys. I didn't have a lot of friends. I also struggled my whole life with having a voice or worse yet, feeling that anyone was listening when I was talking. This poem stems from the dark place I felt I lived for many years. It also tells of the dream to find someone who would care enough to listen. Early on, satan, the enemy of my life was setting me up to fall victim to the first person who showed me any amount of kindness.

Stages: I love this poem. This is the first of my poems that my father understood. As a young man I desperately desired a connection with my father. Our interests were very different. After many failed attempts to connect with my father, I did what many young men who struggle with same sex attractions do, I emotionally detached from him. I put up walls to prevent myself from being hurt further. When he read this poem, he said he completely understood surrender. This poem, like many others was written in the fires of hopelessness. I saw other guys struggling with their sexuality as well. I knew their pain. I believed there was no way out. That thought generated empathy for others and sadness for myself. I honestly believed that I was created by God to help guys come out of the closet. Now I can see that satan was twisting my true calling. I am reminded of Joseph in Genesis 50:20 "You intended to harm me, but God intended it for good to accomplish what is now being done, the saving of many lives." My true calling is to help guys walk away from homosexuality. I wrote this poem as a way of softening the blow of the hopelessness I felt. It also serves to warn others of the struggles that lay ahead with their homosexual desires.

Goodbye: I wrote this as a way of coping with my grandmother's death. When I was younger I was super connected with her. I called her Granny. She was my mom's mother. She used to make lunch for my cousin and I every day while we were in high school. She would sometimes hand me a twenty-dollar bill and call it Hamburger Money. She was the nice grandmother. I don't think my dad's mom liked me all that much. Her real name was Dorothy Nadine Williams. I wrote this poem from her perspective. It helped me with the grieving process.

Bedside Diary: The guy I was dating, at the time, had a longtime friend commit suicide. I didn't know her, but I could sense the pain that he was feeling. At some point he shared the first two lines of her suicide note. I wrote this note for him, a few days after her death. It was my gift to my friend to help him with the grieving process.

Frightened Child: As I aged, I learned more about the development of homosexuality in my own life. This allowed me vision to see the roots of same sex attraction in other people's lives as well. Many in the gay community believe we are born gay. I don't hold to that belief. I have traced its roots in my own life. I have seen many sensitive, young men develop homosexual attractions after having grown up with an overbearing mother and distant father, like me. This poem represents the collective stories of young men in my life who struggle homosexually. There are always common themes in the lives of strugglers. This poem was written because of my attractions, my desire to help others and a fear that ultimately, there was nothing anyone could do.

the chill of a faded whisper: This poem is based on 5 months worth of penguin keeper and penguin observations.

The Passage: I spent many years working as a dolphin trainer. My third day on the job we lost a dolphin named Scooby. I didn't have time to get to know Scooby. The trainers that had worked with him related the things I knew about him, to me. I wrote this poem for them.

Fracture: I wrote this poem for my mom. We had such a strong connection when I was growing up. There was a point in my life that I had to lessen that connection, because it was unhealthy. My closeness to my mother fostered the development of some very feminine characteristics in my life. I learned her moods, her likes, dislikes. I acted like her. I walked and talked like her. I learned how to be a human, by watching my mom. I wrote this poem to let her know that I still loved her, but I needed my space to grow and learn how to be a man. I needed to do this outside of the influence of my mother's shadow. I call this poem 'Fracture', because there was no simple way to lessen our connection without something being broken in the process.

I Died Today: I would hesitate to call this revenge poetry, but it probably is. I wrote this a few days after a bad break up. I was devastated. I retreated to the computer to get my feelings out. I remember feeling a huge sense of relief after I wrote the last line. Among the other emotions I was feeling as I wrote, betrayal seemed all too real to me. I used the keyboard to sentence my anger to solitary confinement in the binary world instead giving it continued freedom in my head.

Images: I promise I have never taken hallucinogenic drugs. That is all I have to say. This piece came about as a result of thinking of the contrasting images of good and evil.

Familiar Strangers: This poem came about because my father was sharing Jesus Christ with my uncle. My uncle was gay and had a partner most of my life. My dad felt led by God to share Jesus with my uncle. My dad said that God gave him a vision of a man who was surrounded by friends, but was still extremely lonely. This to me was the perfect description of my gay life. I always fought hard to be the most popular guy in the room, but at great detriment to my heart. I craved the attention, but was afraid to let people see the real me. I felt they wouldn't like me. I was desperate for friends, so I gave them what I thought they expected. I performed. They applauded. Loneliness grew. And I secretly resented them, because I felt I couldn't share the real me with them. This poem and the next [*eyes of sovereignty*] have similar themes.

The Guardian: There is a lake in the Oklahoma City area that a guy took me to once. My soul always feels refreshed around oceans and lakes. The wind was perfect that night. It danced across the surface of the lake, giving a slight chill to the evening. The cars on the highway were visible, but silent. I sat on the wall surrounding the lake and felt what I know now was the presence of God. Back then I just knew that the place made me feel good for the first time in a long time.

A Cure For Writer's Block: My mom used to write poetry. She said my dad discouraged her from pursuing it further. I am not sure how true of a recollection it was on her part. I wrote this poem about a writer who is plagued by an unknown voice of discouragement and how the writer manages his foe.

Midwater Madness: I wrote this poem to detail a portion of the battle I fought daily with same sex attractions. The poem starts off as a dialogue between two beings observing my fight. I feel like this piece of work is really a microcosm of the great spiritual battle that goes on in a person's life who deals with same sex attractions. On the one hand, I knew that homosexuality was biblically wrong. Yet, I still knew how I had never chosen to be gay. This poem is a representation of my daily battle against my same sex desires and a worldview that says I should embrace my gay identity and be who God "created" me to be. It is about being triumphant over my sin.

Redemption: This poem was birthed from severe writer's block. Or so I thought. I wrote this to get the creative juices flowing. I was going to throw this poem out. Something told me to save it. Many years later, God used the fifth stanza to prophesy into my life. One night my father and I began to talk about how he felt about me. He told me that he didn't love my brother more than me. I had believed that lie my entire life. This new truth was the emerging story that cleansed me from the lies of satan. That night, the foundation of my same sex attractions took a huge hit. I remember God asking me that night what I was going to do now that most of my life had been built on a lie. God used this prophetic poem to reveal the fact that He was in control of my future all along.

Samson's Song: Samson was a baby sea lion that passed away during my first year as an animal trainer. He was an awesome little guy.

Hibernation: I was talking with one of my spiritual mentors about how I felt like I was going nowhere. He told me that at times in our growth we reach plateaus. God will let us rest there awhile and reflect. I wrote this poem shortly after that conversation. I know my mentor had said that it is a time of reflection of previous growth, but it felt more to me, like a cloud of confusion. I saw the world around me speeding forward as I was spinning my wheels.

Who Do You Trust?: Saying that I have trust issues, is like saying Steve Jobs made a lot of money. I was a very sensitive and naïve child. My father punished my brother by spanking, but all he used were stern words to keep me in line. My trust "reflex" has continuously taken a hit over the years. I don't even know how much I trust people or God these days. Forgiveness should be our common practice, but when you get sliced and diced by the world, trust is the hardest thing to try and maintain.

Cutting the Cord: Ministry to guys walking out of homosexuality can be extremely rewarding or devastatingly heartbreaking. I have been actively ministering to men who struggle with same sex attractions for over 13 years. It's the old "Lead a horse to water..." adage that comes to mind. No matter how much truth you share with someone, if they don't see it or accept it, there isn't much you can do. I know the truth that the Holy Spirit revealed to me about same sex attraction.

He is the only one that can reveal the truth to any of us. That doesn't make it any less difficult when guys choose to turn their backs on the truth and embrace homosexuality. This poem arose out of my disappointments in ministry.

Back Porch Recollections: When I began my walk out of my homosexuality, it was because I wanted to train Killer Whales for Sea World Orlando. I knew that God was the only way that dream was ever going to come true. It had been my childhood dream since I was fourteen years old. I moved home to Oklahoma and spent 1999 recovering from the effects of bad emotional and financial living. I rededicated my heart and life to Christ that year. He gave me so many blessings as well. This poem was written on the "back porch" at the Tulsa Airport Mail Processing Center one night, during one of my breaks. I felt like it was God's way of giving me more than just a little hope for the future.

Remembrance: Many months after I moved to San Antonio, my parents visited and we went to the Alamo. I never knew the detailed story of the Alamo until that day. In the middle of the guided tour, I began to cry as the hopeless story of these brave men unfolded. This story and the following poem are the offspring of the emotions that were stirred in me that day. The theme of this poem is representative of the spiritual battle I fight in my daily Christian walk. As a Christian man who left the homosexual life, I fight daily for my voice to be heard in the world. At one point I claimed to be a gay Christian. When God himself said to me, "I can see the gay in your life, but I can't see the Christian," I began to pursue Jesus Christ. This poem represents the barrage of "enemy" assaults that men like myself face, in the media and in the world, when we claim to have walked away from homosexuality. Biblically, I am following God's design for my life. However, when every news program, TV show and every other movie out there celebrates homosexuality, the days can become stressful. Jesus Christ gave me the strength to walk out of homosexuality on December 22, 1998. Matthew 5:10-12 gives me peace in this battle. "10 Blessed are those who are persecuted because of righteousness, for theirs is the kingdom of heaven. 11 Blessed are you when people insult you, persecute you and falsely say all kinds of evil against you because of me. 12 Rejoice and be glad, because great is your reward in heaven..." I still have a heart for those men and women of the gay community. My ministry and my life are lived in service to them.

Demise in the Face of Freedom: This is simply a more poetic and concise version of *Remembrance*.

Never Love Again: This poem came about when I realized, beyond a shadow of doubt that I was probably gay. I was scared. I didn't want to be gay. At the time it seemed like the worst possible fate to me. I prayed nightly for God to change me or take the feelings away. There were days that I felt less gay than others. I wanted a wife, 2.5 children and the white picket fence. I didn't know what to do. I couldn't tell anyone. I knew my life was going to be dramatically altered. The following paragraph accompanied this poem when I shared it with a friend many years later:

"This poem is older. These are the writings that I began to construct when I thought no one could ever love me. I began to tell myself that I was worth nothing, compounding what I thought most people thought of me. Thank God there were people out there who did care about me. I am alive thanks to them. I have to start writing again. My birth vision awaits. If you read this and freak, don't worry. I am okay. I am in a remembrance type of mood."

Sunrise Confessions: I was deep in the heart of love when I wrote Sunrise Confessions. I was still feeling guilty for dating my long-term boyfriend, but I tried to live the best I could in spite of the guilt. I believed with all my heart that God brought us together. No matter what life I led, I still acknowledged God in my life. He never let me forget about Him.

The Passion of Regret: I have some regrets, but God has brought a great deal of redemption into my life. This reflective poem is more about looking back through the years of my life and realizing I believed a lot of lies. In the end, truth won out.

Ship Lights: I wrote this poem one night during one of my slow shifts as a Valet at the San Luis Hotel in Galveston. I was standing near a bannister in front of the hotel, looking out over the ocean. I could see all these tiny little lights shining back at me across the dark waters of the Gulf. I called a friend and the guy I was dating right after that to come up and visit me. I read them the poem. I loved the poem so much that I wanted to get their opinion of it immediately.

Save the Wounded Souls: When I was young I was forever fearful and contemplative about my future. I tried desperately to be pure and holy before God. I struggled with pornography starting at the age of six, so purity was always just out of reach. My thoughts were always at war with my desire to be a good, Christian kid. This was yet another poem discussing the great dilemma that was homosexuality.

Fraternal Disorder: I was in college when I wrote this poem. I was watching a movie with a friend at our fraternity one night. When the movie ended the guy propositioned me. Even though I was gay, I considered this guy a friend, not a potential sexual partner. It freaked me out. I lectured him like a father would lecture a son who was caught doing something bad. I cautioned him on doing something like that again. This poem came out of that experience.

Do You Love Me?: I tried to imagine what Jesus feels like when he pursues us. My mission in life is to help gay men and women leave homosexuality behind if they desire to do so. I wrote this from the perspective of Jesus as he pursues a Christian guy trapped in homosexuality, maybe even celebrating it. I feel like I was that guy most of my life.

Alias: One might consider this more of a prayer of confession than a poem. I knew that Jesus Christ was my savior. I knew that homosexuality was not God's plan for my life. I knew, I knew, I knew. But getting it from head to heart was so difficult. My feelings were always the great gatekeeper. I lived under the religion of hopelessness for so long. I didn't think God could love someone like me, a gay man. That was a lie from the enemy. God loved me all along. He loves me! He loved me when I was gay, mean, gossipy, disrespectful and bitter. Just because he loved me in all those broken places, didn't mean he wanted me to stay there. If you are a gay man reading this right now, make no mistake, God Loves You! The truth is that homosexuality is not His best for you. Heterosexuality is not the goal for your life either. His best is a relationship with Jesus Christ. You don't have to clean yourself up to come to Jesus. Just come.

In Silence Comes My Energy: I would like to say this is a hyper spiritual poem that God dictated to me in a dream one night when I was riding high on His Spirit. The truth is, I think it was one of those times where I was battling God for top position in my life. I wanted to prove that I could take care of myself. I was always a conquering hero in my writing. I was often a coward in real life. This was one of those moments where I desperately longed to be that strong, confident man that I was attracted to. I wanted to be able to take care of myself and live a life that others envied. It was also one of those moments where I pushed God out to the fringes of my life and proudly exclaimed, "I got this!" I had gone to visit Orlando and try to get my foot in the door at Sea World. God let me think I was in control. He let me get a taste of every aspect of the park and then promptly closed every door that I opened. It was a lesson in humility that I needed. I couldn't appreciate it until a few months later.

Shattered: My mom and I were extremely close when I was a kid. She held a great deal of bitterness and unforgiveness against her parents. She hated men because of the way her father treated her as a child. My mom shared very little about her childhood. She made her best effort to shield us from having a childhood like she had. I love my mom. She did the best she could. While she did protect us from how she felt, that great reserve of bitterness altered her behavior. She would erect walls to protect us. All the walls did was create a massive buildup of hurt, rage and random emotion in her heart. We never knew what would trigger the release; when the pain would breach the walls. Mom would go from sweet to angry in seconds. I learned to put up walls by watching her. I used the skill to "protect" myself from hurt. It only served to further alienate me from the friends I desperately needed in my life. I was prone to emotional outbursts as well. God gave me a sensitive heart as a fail-safe mechanism. I can't stay mad at people for very long. This poem came about one day when once and for all my desire to love people overrode my desire to keep them at a distance.

Blind Ambition: I was counseling a guy who was walking away from his gay life at one point, but he got lonely. He met a guy and started dating. He didn't share his struggle with the guy. It was completely selfish on his part. He engaged someone's heart, ignoring the truth of his convictions. I did the same thing back in the day. I knew it was wrong, but I was lonely and I had an agenda. I wanted to show the world that I could be gay and Christian. I wanted to get married to a guy and prove that was okay as well. On and on the façade went. My boyfriend was simply the canvas on which to paint the masterpiece of my agenda. Thank God he was strong willed. Any other guy would have been crushed under the weight of my influence. I wrote this poem as an apology to Joseph and as a way of confessing my selfish motives.

Release: This is one of my favorite poems about God. I wrote this to describe the general euphoria I was feeling about my relationship with Jesus Christ. I wanted to write a thank you/love note back to God for all He had done in my life. This poem was also a remembrance of where he brought me from, 4 years prior.

Mental Gymnastics: My brain was all over the place when I wrote this. Line number seven is embarrassing, but it makes me laugh. I was a big fan. As funny as it may be for a guy to write line number seven, it is an indication of what I believed about myself. A strong-willed woman raised me. The men in my family were passive. The Estrogen Brigade surrounded me. They ran the family and called the shots. You either got on board or you suffered the wrath. Whether I liked it or not, the role models around me were strong women. In order to live a peaceful life, I followed those in charge, much to my detriment. These words were a laundry list of tasks I wanted to accomplish: ridding myself of homosexuality, living a life of purpose or simply doing something with my life. Hopelessness and laziness battled it out to keep me sedentary a little while longer.

Revenge: I dated a guy named Joseph for about a year. It was by far my longest relationship and his first gay relationship. He broke up with me. I didn't take it well. I wrote this poem using his computer. It was the first of many angry pieces I would pen. I wasn't ashamed of it at the time. In fact, I actually shared the poem with him. Needless to say, he didn't sing my praises. At the time, writing this poem was the best outlet with which to diffuse my anger. I feel remorseful now as I read back over it. It stands to me as the evil I was capable of when Jesus was simply an addendum to my life, rather than Lord of my life. Our breakup came at the worse possible time. I had a huge final that week. My dad was in town to dissuade me from getting "married" to Joseph. The night before my final, Joseph broke up with me, using a Sarah McLachlan song. My writing provided a place of escape. For a solid year I had shared every aspect of my life and body with Joseph. Then suddenly, he didn't want to hear my stories anymore. I went a little bit crazy. This poem was the result of feeling betrayed. Revenge is the only title that was appropriate to communicate the bitterness and nastiness of this collection of words.

Freeze Warning: Most people and animals get all hot and bothered in the spring. Winter was always the time when my carnal desires ramped up to an all time high. I think the cold weather amplified my loneliness by forcing me to stay inside. I didn't have roommates or a lot of friends. The desire to sleep next to a warm body was always higher in the winter. Winter was also the time when I grew nostalgic for old relationships. It was the best and worst time of the year.

Brotherly Love: I remember writing this about my brother or in a letter to him.

House of My Sorrow: This is one poem I wrote for a friend after hearing about his tragic childhood. Tragic events had shaped the person he became and the struggles that plagued him as an adult. He began to question his sexuality. The Holy Sprit led me to share the story of how Jesus Christ delivered me from homosexuality. My friend, like me, was born sensitive, not gay. His life is an example of how childhood sexual abuse and a disconnection from men, is one factor in the development of homosexual desires.

The Ritual: I was a very sensitive kid. Outward shows of emotion in my house were not highly prized. I learned early on that emotions were a sign of weakness. I can't remember at what point I wanted to stop being emotional. I began a process of holding back my sensitive side. I didn't let anyone see the hurt I was feeling. I bottled it all up and kept people at bay with anger, assertiveness and a biting tongue. I had a heart of steel when I finally made it college. I fell for the lie that emotions were a weakness. I locked myself up so tight that the only way I could allow myself to cry was to generate a reason. I would drink and listen to sad music, as a way of suppressing my "resolve" muscle. I never let anyone know about my ritual. I would move my desk over to the window in my dorm room and put my desk on top of it. It was my way of watching the world go on around me. The alcohol and the sad music compounded my loneliness. I wanted friends. I wanted to hang out with people, to do something besides merely existing. I would repeat this event as often as I needed to and go right back to walling off my "toxic" sensitivity.

Assassin: I wrote this poem as a response to the predatory guys who took advantage of my friends and I on those lonely nights. I put myself in a lot of ridiculous situations by drinking way too much. I wrote this poem in response to the sexual and emotional predators out there, who think with their penis rather than with their heart.

Simple Solution: It was so easy to write about what was going on in my life when I was young. I couldn't talk about my pain and confusion, but I could write about it openly. In my journals I answered to no one. It was a safe place with no judgment. There were so many emotions running around in my head. Yet it always seemed as if the bad ones always made an appearance in my writing. In this particular poem I was searching for an end to the confusion I lived with on a daily basis. If I could muster enough willpower or think enough good thoughts, I could alter the course of my fate. I was so alone. I had very few friends, so loneliness often surfaced in my writing as well. My mom kept me close. My dad kept far away. The homosexual desires growing in my life left me always in search of answers and solutions to my plight. Upon writing this poem I was still looking for answers within myself. I hadn't yet turned to Jesus for help.

About the author

Matthew Aaron has been writing for over 2 decades. In the beginning, his writing provided a way of escape from a childhood littered with emotional and physical chaos. More of his modern day work has taken on an inspirational and educational feel, with equal parts satire and cynicism thrown in for effect.

In 1998 Matthew Aaron began his journey out of homosexuality with the divine guidance of Jesus Christ. He had lived as a gay man for 10 years. In January of 2000, he achieved his childhood dream of becoming an animal trainer for Sea World. Over a career spanning 15 years, he worked with Killer Whales, Bottle-nosed dolphins, California Sea lions and Otters. He currently serves as the Full-time Director of Big Fish Ministry (www.bigfishministry.org) in Central Florida.

Matthew Aaron has a passion to help men who struggle with same sex attraction, find Jesus Christ and leave homosexuality behind. This passion is evident in his writing. "I knew my life was about to take a different turn. I had finally swam with a Killer Whale. I was living the dream. Then one day God said to me 'Now that you have accomplished your dream, Let Me show the one I have for you.'"

Matthew has been ministering the gospel since 1999 to men struggling with same sex attractions who, like himself, refuse to accept the "born gay" mentality. He is no stranger to controversy and obediently proclaims the truth of God's word wherever he is called. Matthew Aaron writes a blog titled "Unicorns, Aliens and Bigfoot- My post gay life" (www.mattiewalk.com).

This collection of writing titled "Bedside Diary" represents the trials, tests and triumphs of a shy, Oklahoma kid, who grew up afraid of everything. These writings are the daily processes of finding his voice and ending 35 years of silence.

www.ingramcontent.com/pod-product-compliance
Lightning Source LLC
Chambersburg PA
CBHW061729020426
42331CB00006B/1173